AMERICAN I
War Bir

C000217678

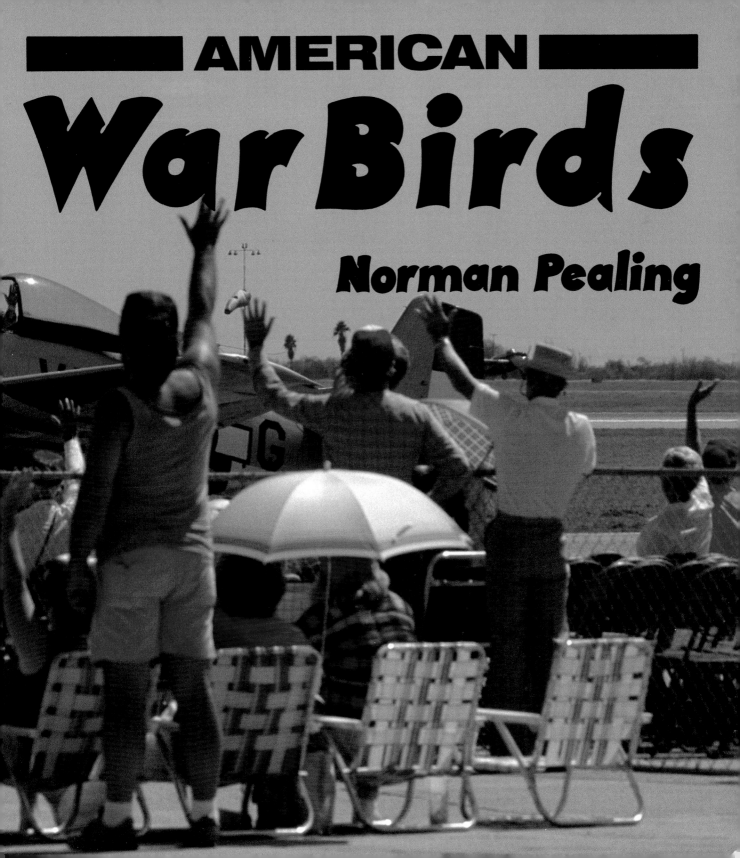

AMERICAN War Birds

Norman Pealing

Published in 1988 by Osprey Publishing Limited
27A Floral Street, London WC2E 9DP
Member company of the George Philip Group

© Norman Pealing

This book is copyrighted under the Berne Convention. All rights reserved. Apart from any fair dealing for the purpose of private study, research, criticism or review, as permitted under the Copyright Act, 1956, no part of this publication may be reproduced, stored in a retrieval system, or transmitted in any form or by any means, electronic, electrical, chemical, mechanical, optical, photocopying, recording or otherwise, without prior written permission. All enquiries should be addressed to the Publishers.

British Library Cataloguing in Publication Data

Pealing, Norman
    American warbirds.—(Osprey colour series)
    1. American military forces. Military aircraft, 1939–1945—
    Illustrations
    I. Title
    623.74'6'0973

ISBN 0-85045-847-1

Editor Dennis Baldry
Captions by Mike Savage
Designed by Martin Richards
Printed in Hong Kong

Front cover The late Stefan Karwowski presents the no-nonsense visage of Stephen Grey's Grumman F8F Bearcat as he formates on the camera ship during a hop from the fighter's Duxford, Cambridgeshire, base. A superlative carrier-based fighter-bomber (or night fighter), the Bearcat was agile, extremely fast (the F8F-2 had a top speed of 447 mph) and, at 5000 ft/min straight off the deck, climbed like the original homesick angel. First flown on 21 August 1944 (XF8F-1) the Bearcat was powered by a Pratt & Whitney R-2800-34W Double Wasp 18-cylinder radial rated at 2400 hp with water injection for takeoff; an extra 400 hp was available if the pilot selected emergency boost

Back cover Dusk settles over Rebel field, a Spitfire, and a pair of BT-13 Valiant trainers at the end of the day's flying

Title pages A Confederate Air Force P-51D Mustang taxies in at Rebel Field, Harlingen, Texas, its pilot responding to well-earned applause at the end of a spectacular performance. In World War 2, US heavy bombers were committed to high-altitude attacks in daylight against Hitler's 'Fortress Europe' after the top brass decided that heavily-armed armadas of B-17s and B-24s could defend themselves against enemy fighters after leaving their short-range shepherds (usually Spitfires and Thunderbolts) behind. The *Luftwaffe* literally shot this idea out of the sky in 1942–43, but the long-range Merlin-engined P-51 transformed everything: here was a fighter which could knock down the deadly swarms of Bf 109s and Fw 190s and escort the bombers all the way to the target and back again. Forty-five years later the Mustang is the world's most numerous warbird

Right Americans and Texans both—as the 'Stars and Stripes' and 'Lone Star' flags proclaim as they flutter over a beautifully restored North American B-25 Mitchell of the Confederate Air Force. One of the great bombers of World War 2, the B-25 was named after Brigadier-General Billy Mitchell, a pioneer advocate of military airpower. Five B-25s and one Navy PBJ-1C now fly with the CAF

Contents

Superfort

Left Visibility from the B-29's cockpit is excellent, especially on the approach. Its hemispherical shape forms the front end of the pressurized crew compartment, the rear of which features a pressure dome—just like today's jetliners. With a service ceiling of 31,850 ft, the Superfortress was a high flyer, making it less vulnerable to interception by Japanese fighters and minimizing fuel consumption

"Fifi" was restored from one of the many derelict B-29s which languished in the desert near the China Lake weapons ränge in California. Prepared for the flight to Harlingen in just nine weeks, the Superfortress made her first flight for 17 years and, 6 hours and 38 trouble-free minutes after leaving China Lake, she touched down at CAF headquarters on 2 August 1971

The first pre-production YB-29 made its maiden flight on 26 June 1943 and it was easily the world's most advanced aircraft, representing a quantum leap in a whole range of technologies, including manufacturing techniques, structures, airborne systems, pressurization, engines, armament and wing loading. Powered by four 2200 hp Wright R-3350-23 Duplex Cyclone 18-cylinder radials with exhaust-driven turbochargers, the B-29 cruised at 290 mph and had a range of 3250 miles with a 10,000 bomb load. The Superfortress was destined for the Pacific theatre where long distance missions were the norm, and the bomber was not

deployed in Europe until after VJ-Day. Initially, B-29s raided Japan from bases in India and China, but later they were able to operate from the Saipan, Guam and Tinian islands when these were captured from the Japanese in 1944

Bottom left Access between the flight deck and fire control centre amidships is by way of a pressurized tube—just big enough to crawl through—which passes over the bomb bays. The fire control system was a radical advance and was entirely remotely controlled. Subsequently, hundreds of B-29s had their four General Electric twin-0.50 calibre machine gun turrets removed to increase speed and altitude performance, leaving only the gunner in the Bell tail turret (equipped with one 20 mm cannon and twin 0.50 calibre guns or three 0.50 calibre guns) for self-defence

Below A particular characteristic of the B-29 is its flat climb out after rotation—not to be mistaken for a laggardly rate of climb—portrayed here as "Fifi" takes off from Harlingen for a re-enactment of the end of the Pacific war in the 1987 Confederate Air Force display. The huge Fowler flaps are electrically driven

The B-29 could carry a maximum internal bomb load of 20,000 lb, but for 'Project Ruby', a joint American-British operation in 1946, three B-29s had their bomb bays specially adapted for what we would today call the semi-conformal carriage of a British 22,000 lb Grand Slam 'earthquake' bomb. Designed by the great Dr Barnes Wallis, this supersonic penetrator had been used with spectacular effect by the Lancasters of No 617 (Dambuster) Sqn near the end of the war, notably against the Bielefeld Viaduct. The modified Superfortresses successfully 'Grand Slammed' the previously invulnerable German submarine assembly plant at Farge and other similar hardened structures. None of the 50 B-29s supplied to help the RAF in 1950–58 (in which service they were known as Washington B.1s) were ever modified to carry Grand Slam

The Superfortress proved beyond doubt that strategic bombing could win wars by neutralizing the enemy's industrial and military capabilities. Even before the specially modified Martin-built B-29s *Enola Gay* and *Bockscar* of Colonel Paul Tibbets' 509th Composite Group delivered the atomic bombs 'Fat Man' and 'Little Boy' over Hiroshima and Nakasaki to end World War 2, massed formations of up to 500 B-29s had laid waste to Tokyo and other Japanese cities and manufacturing centres with a devastating series of fire raids

Right The exceedingly roomy flight deck was a feature much appreciated by tired B-29 crews after ten hours or more on board. Access is via a ladder set up in the nosewheel bay. On the floor between the pilots is a transparent panel to check nosewheel centering. The lady is unforgiving if you neglect to straighten and lock the nosewheel leg before takeoff

Left With his back to the copilot, the flight engineer faced a station on the B-29 which set a standard followed by many a post-war airliner or bomber—jets included. The layout in the B-29 was the first time that the correlation between the duties of the pilots and flight engineer had been thought through on a calculated basis. The result was a reduced workload for all concerned, with better in-flight trouble-shooting and overall improved efficiency

Top right It was lonely on duty in the rear of a B-29, as this unflattering portrait of *"Fifi's"* rear end shows. Also noteworthy in this shot are the big twin mainwheels and double bomb bay. By VJ-Day over 3000 Superforts had been delivered by a production organization comprising Boeing, Bell, North American, Fisher (General Motors) and Martin

Right Silhouetted beneath *"Fifi's"* tail bumper and lower rear remotely-controlled gun turret is *Diamond 'Lil'*, believed to be the last airworthy Liberator. Behind her is a once-in-a-lifetime collection comprising a B-26, an A-26 and a B-25—plus a host of others lined up on the Harlingen ramp. One of the marvellous attributes of the 'guys and gals' who constitute the CAF is their total hospitality and friendliness. They come not only to admire the warbirds of other members but, when the chance comes along, to take a trip in them, too. In August 1987 the caption writer and photographer of this volume had a glorious 40 minutes in a CAF B-17 with the president of Southwest Airlines as a fellow passenger

Bomber force

Daybreak at Harlingen—arguably the most dramatic time of day when ramp activity really hots up—highlights the CAF's very own B-17 Flying Fortress, one of 12,731 examples built between 1935–45. The CAF's Fort is a B-17G, the definitive production version; Boeing churned out 4035 at its Seattle plant, Vega and Douglas adding 2250 and 2395 respectively

Overleaf Once upon an airshow there were two B-17s flying in Britain. Here, *Sally B* formates behind the sister ship now on permanent display in the Bomber Command hall at the Royal Air Force Museum, Hendon. Some of its low-life parts and 1200 hp Wright Cyclone R-1820-65 nine-cylinder radials were exchanged to keep *Sally B* in flying trim. Based at Duxford, *Sally B* currently maintains a high-profile on the UK airshow circuit 43 years after she rolled off the Lockheed-Vega line at Burbank

Left For old-timers, this picture will undoubtedly bring back powerful memories of the mass daylight raids launched from bases in East Anglia and the southeast of England during World War 2. The B-17G was the most heavily-armed bomber of the war, but all the guns in the world and powerful fighter escort could not prevent many B-17s falling to the often deadly accurate *flak* put up by the German defences

Above The B-17's flight deck is nothing if not cosy! But all controls fall easily to hand and visibility through the windscreen is excellent. During steep turns (e.g. on tight finals or evasive action), the three-quarter roof panels above the flight deck were invaluable. The navigator and bombardier sat below and in front of the captain and copilot, well into the nose

Left Colonel 'Doc' Hospers—he is a physician from Dallas—in his B-17 *Chuckie*, resplendent in polished aluminium. It is his own personal transport. Here he taxies for takeoff after a visit to the Confederate Air Force at Harlingen, where the 'Ghost Squadron' celebrated its 30th anniversary in 1987

Below This piratical design incorporates the barrels of the four 20 mm cannon carried in the nose of the Douglas A-20G Havoc. First flown on 26 October 1938 (Douglas 7B), the Havoc was a versatile, hard-hitting aircraft. The French government ordered 100 DB-7s in February 1939 and the first of these went into action against the invading German forces on 31 May 1940. After the fall of France, the few DB-7s which escaped to Britain were supplanted by fresh deliveries to the RAF and these were used in both bomber (as the Boston) and night fighter roles. Interestingly, RAF pilots who flew the French A-20s diverted to Britain had to grapple with metric instrumentation and throttles which operated in the opposite sense (i.e. forward to throttle back and vice versa)

Below War—what war? A sight inconceivable 45 or so years ago! The CAF's B-17 in company with one of the 'Ghost Squadron's' *Kate* torpedo bombers and three *Zeke* replicas. These last four—with others—faithfully represent the 'baddies' at the annual re-enactment of the attack on Pearl Harbor. As one hardened veteran was overheard to say at the spectacle in Texas: 'Jeez, it's more scary here than those two hours in the Pacific all those years ago!' As for the B-17 (which plays the part of a crippled 'Fort' in the demonstration) a comment by General Curtis Le May about the 8th Air Force daylight bombing missions over Germany: 'None were ever aborted or turned back by enemy fighters or *flak*'

Below The Havoc certainly lived up to its name during operations against Field Marshall Erwin Rommel's *Afrika Corps* in the North African campaign of 1942–43, when aircraft of the US Army 9th Air Force bombed and straffed the troops and impedimenta of 'The Desert Fox' across Morocco, Tunisia, and what we know today as Libya. Later, the 9th Air Force used their Havocs with similar success to help nullify the Axis defences before the Normandy invasion

Right All the later marks of Havoc, including the A-20G seen here, were powered by Wright GR-2600 Cyclone 14-cylinder radials of up to 1700 hp. Production had reached 7385 of all marks when production was terminated in September 1944. A total of 3125 A-20s were supplied freely to the Soviet Union during World War 2

Left Havoc with a hammock. Not a shot from a CAF holiday brochure, but a veteran 'Colonel' reflecting(?) on the Havoc's glorious past. It was found forgotten and ailing in Boise, Idaho, with engines not run for 12 years. All of its fabric control surfaces were completely rotten. After many months of restoration it was very cautiously flown to Rebel Field and faithfully restored in the colours of south-western Pacific units and the 312th Bomb Group based in New Guinea, where swashbuckling low-level anti-shipping operations became their calling card with the Japanese

Above The CAF's LB-30B transport, *Diamond 'Lil'*, is steadily being converted to B-24 bomber configuration. Delivered to the RAF as AM927, this is the world's oldest surviving Liberator, being the 24th off the production line. Post-war, it was rebuilt by manufacturer Consolidated as a decidedly roomy corporate transport. An original Liberator nose section (almost certainly from a Navy PB4Y) has already been installed and the current 'civil' rear end is next on the list of modifications. Anyone got a spare Consolidated or Motor Products tail turret?

Above The Liberator was built in greater numbers than any other American warplane: production ended on 31 May 1945 at number 19,203—excluding another 1800 equivalent aircraft built as spares. The production organization was a masterpiece—it had to be—with huge plants like Willow Run (Ford) and Fort Worth (Consolidated, where you'll now see F-16 Fighting Falcons coming off the line), injecting vast numbers of aircraft into the war effort. The tireless men and women on the production tracks produced not only 10,208 bomber versions (the B-24G, H and J), but LB-30A and C-87 transport versions, C-109 fuel tankers to supply B-29s in China, TB-24 trainers, CB-24 lead ships and F-7 photo-reconnaissance aircraft

Right The earliest 'Libs' were judged too immature for combat operations in Europe, so the type was initially employed by the RAF Atlantic Return Ferry Service as LB-30A transports in the spring of 1941. This trailblazing led to the Liberator I for RAF Coastal Command, which was equipped with top secret ASV radar and armed with fixed 20 mm Hispano cannons in the nose. Later, PB6Y-1s (RAF: Liberator IV) of the US Navy and Coastal Command made a tremendous contribution to the Allied victory in the Battle of the Atlantic by sealing the mid-Atlantic patrol gap, previously an important haven and assembly area for 'Wolf Packs' of German U-boats. The B-24C bomber entered service with the US Army in November 1941, shortly before the Japanese pre-emptive strike at Pearl Harbor

Left As its long span, high aspect ratio Davis wing implies, the B-24 Liberator was designed as a long-range, high-speed bomber for the USAAF. The XB-24 prototype made its maiden flight on 29 December 1939. After the war many Liberators were converted for passenger use, especially in Latin America. In the late sixties this caption writer flew in one such B-24 on a midday scheduled flight from Mexico City. The takeoff run at that altitude was decidedly underwhelming!

Below One of many B-25s at Rebel Field taxies past a galaxy of C-47s, an Airacobra and Kingcobra, a Bearcat, P-51s, a 'Messerschmitt Bf 109' and more! The J model seen here (the most numerous version, accounting for 4318 of 9816 built), is powered by two Wright R-2600-29 Cyclone 14-cylinder radials with an original wartime emergency rating of 1850 hp

Right B-25s lined up at Rebel Field before the exciting re-enactment of Lieutenant Colonel Jimmy Doolittle's heroic 18 April 1942 raid against Tokyo and other Japanese cities from the carrier USS *Hornet*. Amazingly, all sixteen Mitchells made successful free take-offs from the carrier at maximum gross weight

Left The distinctive 'gull-wings' of the Mitchell came about as a result of the need to improve directional stability by eliminating dihedral outboard of the engine nacelles. Whatever the aerodynamic reasoning, the modification gave the B-25 a much more purposeful appearance

Left *Yellow Rose* must have been a Texas lady often taken into battle on this B-25. I hope her cowgirl boots and stetson helped the *good ole gal* maintain some sort of decorum in times of stress . . .

Top right The twin-finned tail—here decorated with an American Indian chief—is a recognition feature of the B-25

Right This beguiling B-25 lady certainly did her very special *Show Me* routine over many enemy targets, bagging three Japanese fighter pilots (whose concentration must have been momentarily diverted) into the bargain

Overleaf As the sun rises on another day that promises to do good things for Budweiser stockholders, the heady delights of looking and listening on the Harlingen ramp become apparent. A Mitchell coughs into life, producing a rich-mixture smoke haze—can't you just smell it! Only big radials can sound like this, as *Devil Dog* quivers expectantly on her fat tyres before the pilot eases off the brakes, adds a touch of throttle, and rolls the bomber towards the taxiway

Above *Dagger dagger dagger!* Has the enemy drawn a bead of this taxying B-25? Not in an Avenger, we hope. It's merely a spirited flyby from a navalized Confederate

Right This magnificent Douglas A-26 Invader came all the way from Canada to attend the Confederate Air Force's 30th anniversary at Harlingen. Of such stuff are true believers made! With one of the longest service lives of

any American combat aircraft, the A-26 was designed, developed and produced within the World War 2 timeframe, flying for the first time as the XA-26 on 10 July 1942 and making its debut with service units in December 1943. When the Martin B-26 Marauder was withdrawn from service in 1948, the A-26 was redesignated as the B-26

Above Upward-opening cockpit roof halves are a characteristic of both the Douglas A-26 Invader and the Martin B-26 Marauder. This is *Carolyn*, the only Marauder currently maintained in airworthy condition from a wartime production run of 5266 aircraft

Right Nearly 2500 Invaders had been built when the whole programme was terminated after VJ-Day, the final delivery occuring on 2 January 1946. The Invader's service record in World War 2 was exemplary, dropping 18,000 tons of bombs in 11,000 sorties for the loss of only 67 aircraft. It went on to serve with distinction in the Korean War of 1950–53 and, remanufactured by On Mark as the B-26K (A-26A), performed night interdiction sorties along the Ho Chi Minh trail in Vietnam. The A-26A could carry a warload of 11,000 lb at 350 mph and loiter for two hours in the target area

Left Owned and operated on behalf of the Confederate Air Force, *Carolyn* returns from its display after playing its part in celebrating the 30th anniversary of the 'Ghost Squadron' at Harlingen in 1987. This sexy lady was acquired in 1967 as a distinctly tired corporate transport, and in 1975 the CAF formed the 'B-26 Squadron' under Colonel Jerry Harville. A total of nine years and $250,000 later, *Carolyn* was rightfully restored to Army Air Corps configuration

Below Right from the start of its service career, the B-26 was regarded as a hot ship thanks to its high wing loading and abundant power. Training accidents were high and 'The Window Maker' came to be feared by inexperienced pilots. In the right hands the Marauder presented few problems, but Martin bowed to the inevitable and extended the wing span and vertical tail. In May 1943 the modified B-26B was introduced to the 9th Air Force in Europe and the Marauder rapidly dispelled any remaining doubts about its safety record and operational suitability. By VE-Day B-26 units had suffered combat losses of less than one per cent—the lowest loss rate of any US Army bomber in Europe

Left Tail sting: in common with many other American bombers, the B-26 was armed with a pair of 0.50 calibre Browning machine guns in a powered tail turret

Above The Lockheed PV-2 Harpoon was a redesigned version of the undistinguished Ventura bomber built for the RAF in 1941–42. One of the 'limited editions' of World War 2, only 535 Harpoons were built, but as a long-range torpedo bomber for the US Navy the aircraft was used with considerable success in the South Pacific theatre. Richard and Maggie Mitchell spotted *Fat Cat* as a derelict hulk just off the runway at Marianna Airport, Florida in August 1984. After a superb restoration effort, *Fat Cat* took to the skies again in March 1985

Unlike the Ventura bomber, the PV-2 Harpoon was heavily armed. Up to ten forward-firing 0.50 calibre guns could be carried in the nose and 4000 lbs of bombs or torpedoes internally, plus a further 2000 lbs of stores under the wings. With this warload the Harpoon had a range of about 1800 nautical miles cruising at between 125–135 mph and allowing for acceleration to around 300 mph for combat

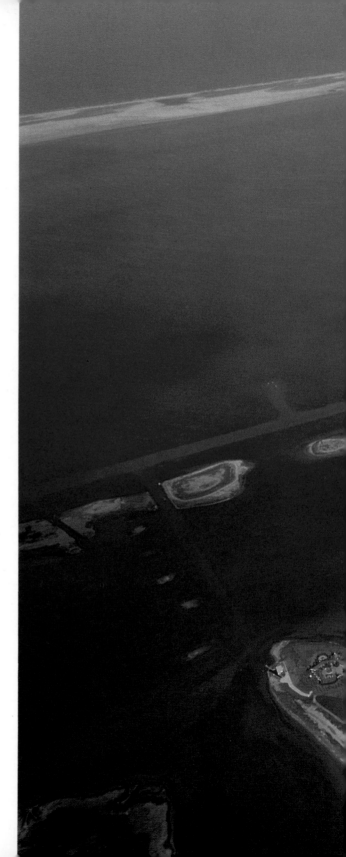

The Harpoon was also used as a make-do long-range fighter in the Pacific and claimed the destruction of a number of Zero-Sens. Other interesting duties included fighter-bomber escort for Army B-24s in the Aleutians as well as C-47s on paradrop missions in New Guinea

Deceptively large with a wing span of 54 ft 2 in and weighing up to 17,895 lb (TBM-3E), the Grumman TBF/TBM Avenger was the US Navy's standard carrier-based torpedo bomber in World War 2. The Avenger had a literal baptism of fire when, on their first mission in the Battle of Midway in June 1942, five aircraft from VT-8 were shot down by Japanese fighters; the sixth Avenger in the formation returned to the USS *Hornet* as scrap metal with a dead gunner. Happily, this mission was totally untypical and the Avenger went on to fly supreme for the remainder of the Pacific war, sending (amongst others) the great super battleship *Musashi* to the bottom. In addition to destroying the Japanese Imperial Fleet, the Avenger and its legendary partner, the SBD Dauntless, despatched millions of tons of Japanese merchant shipping

The Avenger enjoyed a long and productive career with the US Navy and Marines. After the final example rolled off the production line in September 1945, many Avengers were rebuilt to serve in a variety of roles, including anti-submarine warfare (ASW) as the TBM-3E; airborne early warning (AEW) as the TBM-3W and -3W2; target-towing tug as the TBM-3U; carrier on-board delivery (COD) as the TBM-3R; and TBM-3Q ECM platform. Special night attack versions (TBM-3E and 3N) were also produced

Left With a top speed barely above 260 mph the Avenger is obviously no speedster, but with a big reliable 1700 hp Wright R-2600 Cyclone 14-cylinder radial up front and solid, predictable handling, the aircraft makes light(ish) work of formation flying

Top right The business end of the CAF's CASA-built He 111 bomber: the glazed nose conferred superb visibility for the pilot and bomb-aimer cum gunner, but made them vulnerable to head-on attacks by fighters. **Bottom right** The Heinkel's copilot prepares to 'lock in' the greenhouse cockpit of this classic bomber

Left The visitor on the right was a bomb-aimer in He 111s during the war and he is no doubt regailing his host with a tale or two. Although it remained vulnerable to fighter attack after 1940, the He 111 was generally highly regarded as a flying machine, possessing few vices that mattered and being pleasant to handle. The He 111H was the major production version and it was this aircraft which CASA decided to build under licence for the Spanish Air Force

Above The CAF's CASA C.211D prepares to taxi out for takeoff. CASA switched to the Rolls-Royce Merlin engine after supplies of the Junkers Jumo 2111F-2 dried up after 1945. The Heinkel He 111 remained in production in Germany until 1944

This page and overleaf *Luftwaffe* flyby at the CAF airshow in 1987: a Messerschmitt Me 108 Taifun flies wing on the CASA 2111. The shapely Taifun served with the *Luftwaffe* and German Army as a liason and courier aircraft and was the precursor to the Bf 109 fighter

Right Break! A Heinkel, Spitfire and Messerschmitt in close proximity over Texas—a real crowd pleaser

Hot pursuits

One of the greatest fighters in history, and arguably the most outstanding combat aircraft to emerge from World War 2, the North American P-51 Mustang was the breathtaking result of an April 1940 agreement between the British Air Purchasing Commission and the great 'Dutch' Kindelberger, chairman of North American Aviation, for the design and development of a new fighter for the RAF. NAA took just 117 days to design and build the NA-73X prototype, which made its maiden flight on 26 October 1940 following a six week delay while Allison struggled to deliver their new V-1710 vee-12 engine. The rest, as they say, is history. Here, Stephen Grey puts his P-51D *Moose* through its paces in the vicinity of North Weald during the 1986 'Fighter Meet'

Left P-51D *Gunfighter II* en route to the runway at Rebel Field. The Packard 1590 hp V-1650-7 Merlin-engined D model was by far the most numerous version of the Mustang, outnumbering all the other models combined. A grand total of 15,586 Mustangs were delivered

This page Three Merlins and an Allison: P-51Ds follow a P-40 as they thread their way along the taxiway at Harlingen, the sound of their vee-12 engines sweet music to thousands of spectators. P-40F/Ls were also powered by Packard Merlins

Left A quartet of immaculate P-51Ds taxi out at the 1987 Confederate Air Force display. General Eisenhower was so impressed with the Mustang that he flew over the Normandy beachhead in a specially modified example flown by Major General Elwood 'Pete' Quesada

Above Nose art was by no means confined to bombers, nor only used as a reminder of the crew's more basic fantasies! *Death Rattler* represented a truism in Mustang terms—many a German and Japanese pilot came to rue the day he mixed it with a P-51

Old Crow crackles past, showing to good effect the Mustang's wide track landing gear made possible by the neat inward-retracting gears. This is obviously a much better arrangement than the outward-retracting gears found on aircraft like the Spitfire and Bf 109, whose pilots had to contend with a very narrow main track which hardly helped to contain the swing caused by powerful engines on takeoff and landing; on some of the more rudimentary front-line airfields taxying was distinctly taxing

Presumably a chequerboard tailplane on your
P-51 comes in handy for a quick game of chess
during those long hours at dispersal. The
Mustang was not a comfortable aircraft to fly on
those oh so long escort missions and the
cockpit was noisy and cold at extreme altitudes.
Yet few would have changed it for anything
other than a later mark (except the squirrelly
lightweight H model)

Left Sporting distinctive Normandy invasion stripes, this view of a P-51D—the very one flown at Harlingen by a certain Brigadier-General 'Chuck' Yeager—shows off its big four-bladed, blunt-tipped Hamilton Standard propeller. The D model had a top speed of 437 mph and packed six 0.50 calibre Browning MG53-2 machine guns in the wings fed by 270 or 400-round magazines each

Below The P-51D introduced a beautiful teardrop hood which transformed visibility from the cockpit. Many earlier models were refitted with a bulged sliding Malcolm canopy of British design

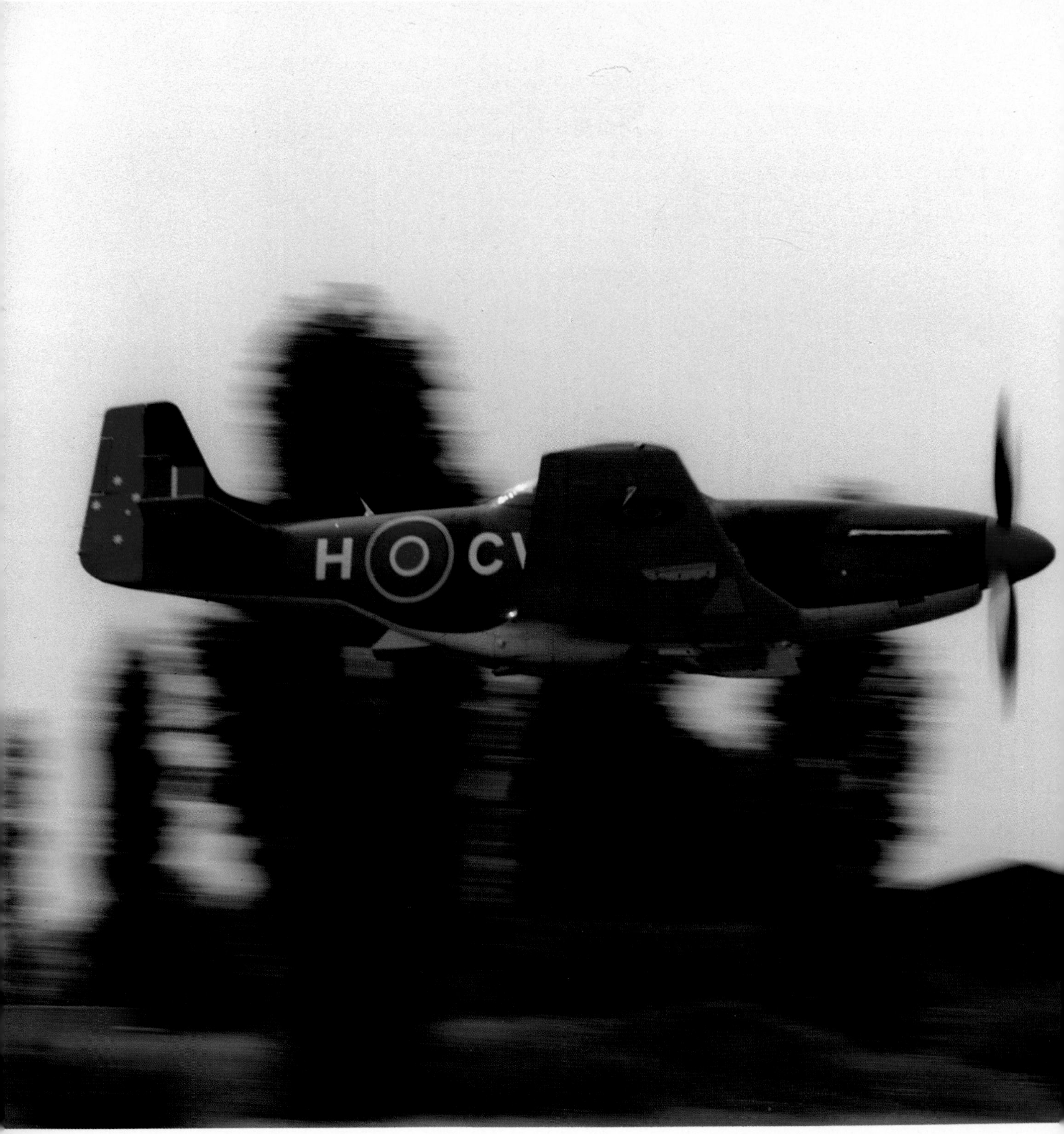
H
CV

Left Ray Hanna—an ex-leader of the RAF's Red Arrows formation aerobatic team—takes The Old Flying Machine Company's P-51D down for a close encounter with the main runway at North Weald during the 1987 'Fighter Meet'. This Mustang was built under licence in Australia by the Commonwealth Aircraft Corporation and bears the attractive markings of No 3 Sqn, RAAF, which operated P-51s in Italy during 1944–45

Right Another design masterpiece from North American Aviation, the F-82 (post-1948 designation) Twin Mustang would have escorted the high flying B-29s all the way from their bases in China and the Pacific islands to targets in Japan and back again had the war continued beyond 1945. After the A-bomb attacks on Hiroshima and Nagasaki the Army Air Force promptly cancelled some 480 of the 500 P-82Bs on order. Created by joining two P-51 fuselages at the wings and tailplane, the prototype XP-82 made its maiden flight on 15 April 1945. The AAF subsequently secured a trickle of post-war deliveries, production reaching the 400-mark with the advent of the F-82G night fighter equipped with SCR-720 search radar

Bottom right The P-82E day escort model (100 built) also had a useful attack capability, armed with six 0.50 calibre machine guns in a detachable tray, plus a 4000 lb bomb load or 24 5-inch air-to-surface rockets. The Twin Mustang saw considerable action in Korea, where Lt Hudson of the 68th Fighter Squadron in his P-82B gained the distinction of scoring the first kill of that conflict (also the first Air Force victory). Most Twin Mustangs served with Air Defense Command. The P-82 seen here was in airworthy condition when it attended the 1987 Confederate Air Force airshow, but a landing accident after its display caused serious damage to the propellers, landing gears and airframe. Fortunately the crew were able to walk away from the crash and the owner's have pledged to restore this fascinating aircraft back to flying condition. The cost of repairs is estimated at $300,000

Left An extremely advanced warplane at the time of its first flight on 27 January 1939, the Lightning was Lockheed's bold response to a February 1937 US Army Air Corps specification for a long-range pursuit and escort fighter capable of sustaining 360 mph for one hour at 20,000 ft. The P-38 featured a string of hi-tech items, including a tricycle landing gear, Fowler flaps and the new Allison V-1710 vee-12 glycol-cooled engine with GEC turbos recessed into the tail booms, cooling radiators on the sides of the booms and induction intercoolers in the wing leading edges. The beautifully streamlined central nacelle accommodated the powerful nose armament and pilot

Right 'Lefty' Gardner and his P-38 *White Lit'nin* are firm favourites at Harlingen and the Reno air races. Gardner's superbly crafted display is certainly on the 'unmissable' list of every airshow devotee

Although less manoeuvrable than contemporary single-engined fighters, the P-38 endeared itself to pilots by proving to be exceptionally reliable, long-ranged, hard-hitting and fast—up to 414 mph in later versions. When the US declared war on Japan and Germany on 7 December 1941 one hot shot P-38E pilot lost no time in drawing first blood, destroying a snooping Fw 200C Condor near Iceland within a few minutes of the announcement. The Condor stood little chance against the E model's battery of one 20 mm Hispano cannon, four 0.50 Browning and two Colt 0.30 calibre machine guns. This armament was standard on most P-38 models. Another notable kill for the P-38 came when 16 aircraft of the 339th Fighter Squadron shot down Admiral Yamamoto's G4M transport after flying 550 miles from their Guadalcanal base

Left Menacing sharkmouths were a feature of many P-40 Warhawks. The P-40 achieved immortality through the exploits of Major General Claire Chennault's American Volunteer Group, 'The Flying Tigers'. The three squadrons which defended Chinese airfields and supply lines between December 1941 and 4 July 1942 racked up 286 kills against Japanese fighters and bombers for the loss of 23 US pilots. Since the Warhawk could never match the Zero-Sen's speed, agility and ceiling, Chennault perfected unorthodox hit-and-run tactics, capitalising on the aircraft's ruggedness, weight, superior diving qualities and the fighting prowess of his pilots

Below How low can you get—and what's the propeller clearance?! Ray Hanna knows, that's why he flies The Old Flying Machine Company's Curtiss P-40 Kittyhawk with the touch of the master. Although generally outclassed by enemy fighters, the P-40 Warhawk family (the name Kittyhawk was only applied to aircraft delivered to the RAF), proved particularly adept in the close support role. Aggressively flown by RAF pilots in the Western Desert, the P-40 was a constant threat to German motorized columns and troops in the open. Nearly 14,000 Warhawks had been produced when the final delivery (a P-40N) took place in March 1944

Preceding pages Used in large numbers by the US Army Air Force and the Soviet Air Force, the unconventional Bell P-39 Airacobra was unique in having a nosewheel-type landing gear and the 1325 hp Allison V-1710-63 vee-12 behind the pilot. The propeller drive shaft ran under the pilot's seat and the reduction gearbox was located in the nose. Most P-39s were armed with a 37 mm cannon firing through the propeller hub, two 0.50 calibre machine guns in the nose synchronized to fire past the propeller and two 0.30 calibre machine guns in the outer wings

Top right The perfectly streamlined bubble canopy sets off this close up portrait of the biggest, most powerful single-engined fighter to see combat in World War 2—the mighty P-47 Thunderbolt of 'Jug'. The crowning masterpiece of Republic's chief designer, Alexander Kartveli, the P-47's juggernaut proportions were determined by the massive Pratt & Whitney R-2800 Double Wasp 18-cylinder two-row radial (which grew in output from 2000 hp in the B model to 2800 hp in the P-47M/N), the bulky rear fuselage turbo and formidable eight gun Browning armament

Bottom right *No Guts No Glory!* The Thunderbolt pulverized the Axis throughout the European, Pacific and Far East combat zones, straffing, bombing, rocketing and proving a surprisingly agile fast-climbing dogfighter. Production totalled 15,660, including a staggering 12,603 D models from Republic's Farmingdale (which, thanks to the demise of the Fairchild T-46 Air Force trainer, no longer manufactures aircraft) and Evansville, Long Island plants. It's hard to believe that so many aircraft can simply disappear, but when the Confederate Air Force began searching for P-47s in the late sixties they failed to find a single example in airworthy condition

Far right More Spitfires were built—over 22,000—than any other Allied warplane. The CAF's Spitfire Mk IX proudly bears the personal codes and wing commander's pennant of the British legless fighter ace Douglas Bader

Above A Spitfire, 'Messerschmitt Bf 109' and P-40 together? Unthinkable in the dark days of war, but commonplace at Harlingen today

Right The CAF's ex-Spanish Air Force HA.1112 Buchón (a licence built Bf 109G) makes the same noise as a Spitfire because it too has a Rolls-Royce Merlin up front. CASA-built 109s shared the awkward sideways-opening heavily framed canopy of the G model (as here), but many were fitted with clear-vision Galland hoods. Interestingly, CAF pilots were contracted to fly these 109 lookalikes in the epic motion picture *The Battle of Britain* made in 1968

Left and top right The Grumman F4F/FM
Wildcat (or Martlet in British Fleet Air Arm
service) was a marvellous naval fighter—feisty,
solid, dependable and manoeuvrable. They
fought magnificently against the Japanese
onslaught in the Pacific until relieved by the F6F
Hellcat at the end of 1943. Wildcats and Martlets
continued to operate from the smaller escort
carriers until the end of the war

Right The Vought F4U Corsair was a very
different naval fighter to the relatively diminutive
Wildcat, being a real 'muscle plane' with
tremendous power and formidable offensive
capability. Powered by the famous Double Wasp
radial, the XF4U-1 prototype made history by
becoming the first US warplane to exceed 400
mph in level flight. Because of the poor view
over the long nose, the US Navy judged the
Corsair to be unsuitable for carrier operations (a
view not shared by Britain's Fleet Air Arm), and
unusually the Marine Corps accepted all the
early deliveries

Left From the moment the Marines hit the Solomons in February 1943 their Corsairs had the enemy on the run. Demoralized Japanese pilots dubbed the bent wing bird 'The Whispering Death'. The Marines are a determined bunch as one Lt Robert Klingman demonstrated during a combat with a Japanese *Nick* fighter at 38,000 ft. Finding his guns had frozen, he coolly sawed off the tail surfaces of the opposing fighter with his propeller

Below As the beefed up AU-1 the Corsair saw further action in Korea, but by this time the aircraft had lost its fine handling qualities, proving a real handful for the average pilot. The monster F2G was even worse, ploughing behind a 3000 hp Pratt & Whitney R-4360 Wasp Major 28-cylinder four-row radial. Corsair production ended as late as December 1952 at number 12,571

A classic piston-engined 'cat from the Grumman litter, the Bearcat marked the end of a glorious era in fighter design. Bearcats can still be seen rounding the pylons at the Reno races, although they seem to lack the competitive edge seen in previous years. In August 1969 Darryl Greenamyer set a new mark for non-jet aircraft by squeezing 482.5 mph out of a specially modified Bearcat. The P-51D *Dago Red* raised the record to 517.06 mph on 30 July 1983. Stephen Grey's basically stock F8F is also featured on the front cover

Top trainers

Left Even rarer, only to be seen flying at Rebel Field with the Confederate Air Force, is this delightful Focke Wulf Fw 44 Stieglitz. It was developed in 1932 as a primary and aerobatic trainer for the *Luftwaffe*. This is believed to be the world's only airworthy example

Below The Fleet Finch trainer is a rare bird these days, but this pristine example looks good for another sixty-or-so years. As its markings suggest, a few saw RAF service between the wars

In 1939 the US Army Air Corps took delivery of its first low wing monoplane trainer. The Ryan PT-22 Recruit was the shape of wings to come for the USAAC, and was derived from a series of Ryan trainers which began with the ST Sport in 1934. In many ways it was advanced for its time, with disc brakes and a steerable tailwheel

Below A Boeing/Stearman PT-17 Kaydet taxies behind the Ryan Recruit as the trainer pageant unfolds at Rebel Field. The PT-17 entered service as an Army and Navy trainer in the same year that Stearman became a Boeing company—1934. A total of around 10,000 were produced, training more American service pilots than any other aircraft. Post-war, many were bought up dirt cheap and (appropriately enough) used as crop sprayers

Right A vic of BT-13 Consolidated Vultee Valiants fly serenely through the big Texas sky. The 'Vibrator' introduced students to R/T, instrument flying and high-powered Pratt and Whitney radials. These aircraft are based at Odessa, Texas

Above It doesn't look like much of a prop, but can it make a noise! Transonic prop tips and a buzzing Wasp radial combine to make the T-6 an environmental hazard

Right One of the greatest trainers of all time, quite possibly *the* greatest, the classic North American T-6 Texan entered production in 1938 and remained the USAF's basic and advanced trainer until 1956. NAA had built 15,109 T-6s by 1945, and versions were built in Australia as the Wirraway, by Noorduyn in Canada, in Japan (earning the Allied code-name *Oak*) and by Saab in Sweden. Canadian Car & Foundry built 555 T-6Gs in 1951–54 for FAC (forward air control) work in Korea

The prototype of what we know today as the Texan (or Harvard, as it was called by the RAF) began as the NA-16, which first flew in April 1935. The NA-16 was powered by a 400 hp Wright R-975 Whirlwind radial; most T-6s have Pratt & Whitney engines of 550 hp

U.S. AIR FORCE
93350

220218

N49RR

Left Every T-6 must have a tale to tell of lessons learned (or otherwise) and practice hopefully making perfect. No less than 50,000 USAAF pilots, plus another 40,000 from the Navy (their Texans were designated SNJ) learned to fly on this trainer to end trainers. In addition, countless thousands of other fliers from the air arms of 34 foreign nations qualified on the T-6

Bottom right 'He was coming at me like this, see' . . . A group of veteran T-6ers gather rounds *Ms. Hazel* to relive magic moments

Bottom left The T-6 has a maximum speed of 206 mph and cruises at 180 at 11,000 ft. it lands at 66 mph—which was fast in the immediate post-biplane era

Overleaf A great many Texans were left in natural metal finish, like this ex-Royal Canadian Air Force example. Although usually unarmed, the T-6 could be fitted with a 0.30 or .303 calibre machine gun in the right outer wing panel for gunnery practice. Trainee gunners learned how to shoot from the rear cockpit of an AT-6 or SNJ, the rear section of the canopy folding up and over

Above Where better for Texans to roost than Rebel Field, Texas? The Confederate Air Force show is a magnet for T-6 owners and 'Colonels' across the nation

Left Texans make ideal formation display aircraft. Its swept-back wing leading-edge and triangular fin and rudder gives the aircraft a distinctive appearance

Left Michael J Brady is the founder and 'boss' of Northwest Airlink, a leading regional carrier in the US. He likes to relax by flying his beautifully restored Beech T-34 Mentor. Here he taxies out from the general aviation hangar at Harlingen. He bought the T-34 from Fred Smith (the main man at FedEx), since when he has lavished many hours of loving care on the aircraft. Mike's attention to detail was rewarded at Oshkosh in 1987 when his aircraft earned a prize in a competition which he didn't mean to enter!

Above The Bonanza's influence on the design is apparent in this view of the T-34. Beech developed the Mentor as a private venture and the trainer made its maiden flight on 2 December 1948. After being evaluated as the YT-34 in 1950, the USAF placed an order for 350 T-34As, followed by 423 T-34Bs for the Navy. The B45 export model was ordered by Argentina, Chile, Columbia, Mexico, El Salvador and Venezuela. Canadian Car & Foundry built 56, of which 24 were supplied to Turkey. Fuji manufactured 126 under licence for the Japanese Self-Defence Force

Left This Norman Pealing close up taken near Memphis, Tennessee, shows just how roomy the T-34's cockpit is. Flying Mike Brady's Mentor is his assistant chief pilot, Jim Gardner, with your faithful correspondent in back. This aircraft has full dual controls, is fully aerobatic and boasts a host of hi-tech avionics, including colour weather radar. The propeller has recently been chrome plated

The T-34 is powered by a 225 hp Continental O-470-13A 'flat-six' engine, giving a maximum speed of 189 mph at sea level. Some Mentors had 340 hp Lycomings

Like the Harvard, the Beech T-34 makes
a splendid formation aircraft. Here three select
smoke as they fly by over Harlingen

Mike Brady turns final in his T-34—note the
Bonanza-type landing gear

Right Three T-34s in arrow formation under a
perfect sky. The Mentor weighs in at just over
3300 lb at takeoff and has a service ceiling of
26,800 ft. Visibility for both student and instructor
is excellent. With a range of 600 miles, there is
plenty of endurance for a worthwhile training
session

Cargo classics

Popularly known as the Twin Beech, the C-45 Expeditor was one of the most successful and widely-used aircraft of its size and type ever built. It was derived from the Beech Model C-18 of the late 1930s. As the C-45 it became a light cargo and personnel transport and as the AT-11—with a bomb bay carrying ten 100 lb bombs and equipped with a 0.30 calibre machine gun in a dorsal turret—it served as a bombardier and gunnery trainer; the AT-7 version was a navigation trainer. C-45 Expeditors were used extensively as corporate transports after the war and many are still in service in Asia and the Far East. Confederate Air Force C-45s are assigned to wings in New Mexico, Oklahoma and New Zealand

One of the great war winners, the Douglas C-47 Skytrain is a legend and one of the world's best known aircraft. Almost universally known as the Dakota, it survives in considerable numbers. This C-47 is operated by the Confederate Air Force

Right The CAF's C-47 flies in to attend the type's 50th birthday party at Abbotsford, British Columbia in 1986

DC-3s by the yard at Abbotsford, scenes reminisent of the massive airborne operations in World War 2 such as Arnhem and D-Day. When you next stand and gaze at a DC-3 you'd better hope that oil is dripping from the Pratt & Whitneys. As one old hand was heard to say: 'When no oil is leaking, there is none in the engine. You should add some'. No problem!

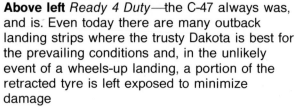

Above left *Ready 4 Duty*—the C-47 always was, and is. Even today there are many outback landing strips where the trusty Dakota is best for the prevailing conditions and, in the unlikely event of a wheels-up landing, a portion of the retracted tyre is left exposed to minimize damage

Above right Despite the streamlined shape of the fuselage extending over the nose (the hull was originally designed for pressurization) visibility from the flight deck is very good. The C-46 did a fantastic trucking job over the 'Hump' route from India to China across the Himalayas, braving 20,000-ft peaks and 100 mph headwinds. No less than 106,000 passengers and 46 million pounds of cargo were carried in one month alone

Right Many aircraft manufacturers have tried to design a 'DC-3 replacement': the Vickers Viking, Saab Scandia, Handley Page Herald, Fokker Friendship and Avro 748 spring to mind. But nobody has ever really cracked the DC-3's secret. Today, even reworked turboprop versions—including one with three engines— are available and certificated. This is *Draggin' Lady*, resplendent in Army Air Corps uniform, waiting to let rip at Harlingen

This page Invasion-striped C-47 departs on a pleasure flying detail

Overleaf *The Tinker Belle* is the CAF's magnificent Curtiss C-46 Commando, a machine which demands 'hands on' attention from the pilots at all times. Once you've mastered the technique, flying the 'Charlie 46' is a very satisfying experience

Of ample proportions—not to say stout—the C-46 is nevertheless an attractive and impressive aircraft. About 3300 were delivered between October 1941 and VJ-Day